Duncan Edwards
A Black Country Colossus

David Barratt, David Harrison & Alan Hughes

Foreword by Ron Atkinson

**Duncan Edwards
A Black Country Colossus**

© David Barratt, David Harrison & Alan Hughes 2023.

This book is copyright under the Berne Convention. All rights are reserved. Apart from any fair dealing for the purpose of private study, research, criticism or review, as permitted under the Copyright Act, 1956, no part of this publication may be reproduced, stored in a retrieval system, or transmitted, in any form or by any means, electronic, electrical, chemical, mechanical, optical, photocopying, recording or otherwise, without the prior permission of the copyright owner. Enquiries should be sent to the publishers at the undermentioned address:

EMPIRE PUBLICATIONS
1 Newton Street, Manchester M1 1HW

© Design: Alan Hughes.

© Additional text: David Harrison.

Acknowledgements

Thanks to Duncan's school friends: Lawson Crewe, Tommy Millinson, Brian Turner, David Partridge and Brian Woodhall.
With gratitude and thanks to Duncan's close family for their help, encouragement and support throughout the years.
We are eternally grateful to all the staff at Dudley Archives for their help and assistance over the past six years.
And special thanks go to Carolyn Price for her input with some of the photos in this book.
Thanks to Jim Cadman, *Express & Star*, Rose Cook Monk, *The Black Country Bugle*
– and Ron Atkinson for kindly contributing his foreword.
A massive thank you to Dave Barratt's Archives 'buddy' and friend
James Hadley for his help, patience and enthusiasm.
Special thanks to Steve Gordos, Chris Brazier and Jo Lateu for kindly proofreading the book.

Dedicated to H Barratt
– we lived it together.

DAVID BARRATT is Tipton born and bred. He attended Park Lane Secondary Modern School
before working as a toolmaker, retiring in 2012. He played amateur football and has been a
West Bromwich Albion supporter all his life. A keen gardener, he lives in Dudley with his wife Elaine.

DAVID HARRISON was born and raised in Tipton and spent most of his working life as a journalist on local and national newspapers, mostly as a sports reporter. He has ghosted several football books for players like Alan Shearer and Michael Owen and co-wrote a biography of Wolves legend Derek Dougan. Now retired, he lives in Tettenhall, Wolverhampton.

ALAN HUGHES was a graphic designer at New Internationalist, Oxford. Born and raised in Tipton he was a sheet metal worker at British Federal, Dudley, for 15 years, before gaining a BA degree in Visual Communications.
He supports Aston Villa FC. Now retired, he lives in Oxford with his dog Satchmo.

ISBN: 978-1-915616-06-7

CONTENTS

Foreword	7
Introduction	9
The Early Years	13
Feet First at School	17
The Lad from Dudley	38
The Other Side of Duncan	41
Grange Park	47
Charles Buchan's Football Monthly	48
The Busby Babes	53
Bobby and Duncan	70
Duncan in Great Company	72
Matt Busby	74
Playing for England	77
Falling in Love	83
You're in the Army Now	85
Death and Disaster at Munich	91
Rest in Peace Duncan	103
In Loving Memory of Duncan	107
The Flowers of Manchester	118

What they say about Duncan Edwards...

"Ask me who is the greatest footballer the world has ever seen. Ask me who is the greatest footballer I ever played with. Ask me who is the greatest footballer I ever played against. Same answer: Duncan Edwards. Don't ask me how much greater he would have become. It defies imagination. What's bigger than a colossus? Think about that. Then remember that I played not only with George Best and Denis Law but with Bobby Moore. That I played against Pele and Maradona. They were truly great, but Duncan was the greatest."
– Bobby Charlton

"If I shut my eyes now I can see him. Those pants hitched up, the wild leaps of boyish enthusiasm as he came running out of the tunnel, the tremendous power of his tackle, always fair but fearsome, the immense power on the ball. The number of times he was robbed of the ball once he had it at his feet could be counted on one hand. He was a players' player. The greatest... there was only one and that was Duncan Edwards."
– Jimmy Murphy

"A wonderful, wonderful footballer who would have gone on to be one of the world's greatest players."
– Alan Hodgkinson

"There will never be another player like him."
– Bobby Moore

Foreword

DUNCAN EDWARDS was rightly hailed as the football giant of his day but let's not forget he was just 21 years old when he died so tragically from injuries he suffered at the Munich air disaster.

For me that begs the question: how great would he have become had he lived, and his career continued to develop at the same astonishing rate?

I will answer that quite simply. He would have been the greatest British footballer of all time – maybe one of the best in the world.

I marvelled at Duncan's brilliance on the few occasions I saw him play. His power with and without the ball was understandable because of his sheer size but he had the skills and goalscoring ability to match.

I will confess here that the most complete player I ever saw was the Welsh wizard John Charles. He was the best centre half in my opinion, and, at the same time, he was a great striker. That's how complete he was. The Welshman could start a game up front, score a couple of goals, then switch back into defence to help keep out the opposition.

It's difficult to pass judgement, but I would not hesitate to suggest Big Dunc would have surpassed him and become even greater. He offered the same versatility as Charles, had the same physical presence. He was great in the air, good with both feet and had an eye for goalscoring.

If we roll on to 1966 and England's World Cup victory against Germany, Duncan would only have been 29 and it doesn't take much to imagine that he would have been in that team, most probably as captain.

The question is: which would have been his best position? Would he have been a central defender in Alf Ramsey's line-up, in which case would that mean he would have sidelined Bobby Moore? Or if he had been a midfielder, would he have played alongside his big pal Bobby Charlton, which would have meant no place for Nobby Stiles?

It's all conjecture, of course, but we only have to listen to those who witnessed his greatness to realise what a colossus he was.

Bobby Charlton had no doubts: "He was the only player who made me feel inferior. I wasn't fit to tie his shoelaces."

And Manchester United assistant manager Jimmy Murphy opined: "When I used to hear Muhammad Ali proclaim to the world that he was the greatest, I used to smile. You see, the greatest of them all was an English footballer named Duncan Edwards."

There have been many such tributes to Duncan but perhaps the greatest tribute of all is that his name, his reputation and the memories of who and what he was are being kept alive after all these years. I can think of no other player who has provoked so much pure affection and admiration so long after his death. Long may it continue.

Like Duncan, David Barratt is Black Country born and bred and has devoted himself to researching Duncan's history. This book – put together with the help of David's old mates David Harrison and Alan Hughes – contains a unique collection of pictures and articles, and illustrates the outstanding, but sadly brief, life of the great footballer from Dudley.

Ron Atkinson

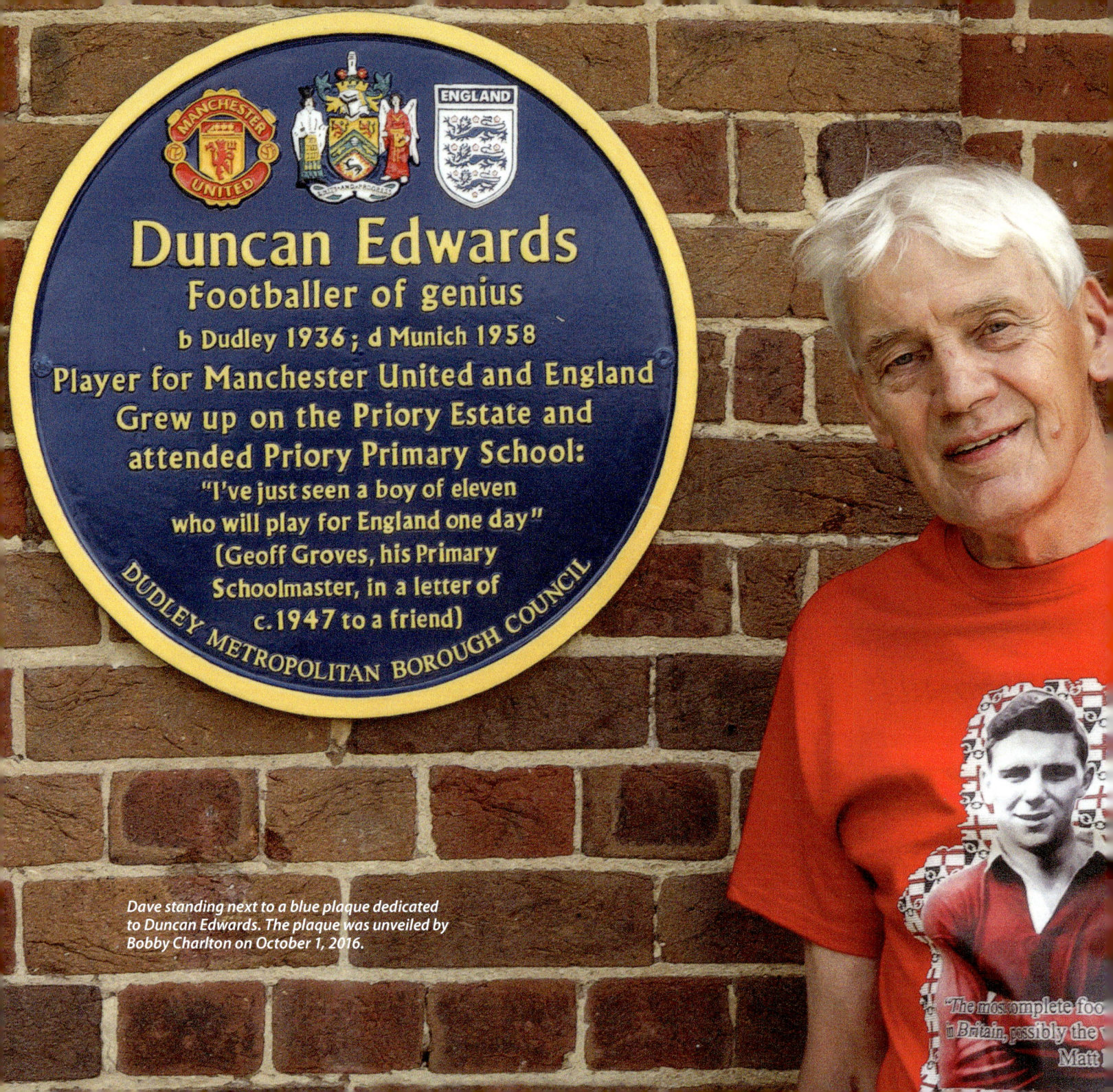

Dave standing next to a blue plaque dedicated to Duncan Edwards. The plaque was unveiled by Bobby Charlton on October 1, 2016.

Introduction

He was five years old when he first became aware of DUNCAN EDWARDS. That was in 1952. But from those distant beginnings DAVID BARRATT developed an interest which was to become a fascination, an obsession and, some might say, an addiction which has lasted over 70 years. This is his story.

BECAUSE OF FAMILY CIRCUMSTANCES, Tipton-born David (Dave to his mates) and his younger brother Harold (who everyone knew as 'H') had to move from the place of their birth to within reach of Duncan Edwards's home on Dudley's Priory Estate.

Dave explains: "I was only five at the time, H was four. We lived in High Street, Princes End, where I was born. It was a two-bedroom house which we shared with other family members. It was somewhat overcrowded so we moved out. My dad worked with a woman at the Sankey's works in Bilston and she offered to let us live with her for a while.

"She put us up for six weeks in Beech Road in Dudley. It was a corner kick away from Duncan's house in Elm Road. We could almost see into his house from where we lived.

"H and I both loved football and all we heard people talk about was this talented young footballer who came from Dudley.

"That was in 1952 and Duncan had already signed for Manchester United. He was just 16 years old. He had also won a lot of England schoolboy caps and all the kids idolised him."

After six weeks in Beech Road, the Barratt family moved back to Princes End and the two brothers went to Burnt Tree School. They did return to the Priory estate briefly in 1955 before they were housed in a block of flats in Latham Crescent, Tipton.

Dave continues: "We lived with the Gray family in Beech Road again and Mrs Gray was like a second mother to us. Her son Johnny went to Wolverhampton Street School with Duncan and that was all he ever talked about. By then everyone knew of Duncan. He had won his first senior England cap, against Scotland, in 1955.

"One of the Gray family was getting married, and H was chosen to be a page boy, wearing the full page boy gear, much to H's embarrassment!

"I will never forget that day. There was a knock on the front door and someone shouted, 'He's back!'

"It was like one of the Beatles had turned up. Everyone dashed down to Priory Park, which was one of Duncan's favourite places. It was where he developed his footballing skills as a kid.

"Anyway, H quickly changed out of his page boy outfit and off we went to the park. Duncan was there kicking and heading a ball around with the kids. A lot of dads joined in as well. There must have been 40 of us there in total. It was a magical moment. Don't forget Duncan was already a full England international and there he was having a kickabout with kids and their dads on Priory Park. But whenever he came back, he never acted like a big star. He was still this young lad from Elm Road. I was in total awe of him."

School photos of Dave (left) and his brother 'H' (below).

Football-fanatic Dave had started to collect bubble gum cards which carried pictures of all the famous footballers of the day. They sold at two old pence a packet and there was 48 in each set. Ironically, the only one missing from Dave's set was Duncan Edwards. He tried everything to get it but no-one was willing to swap. Then one day Mr Whitehouse, his schoolteacher, approached him.

"I have got something for you, Dave," he said. He handed over the treasured picture card of Duncan. By then most people were aware that Dave idolised the Manchester United and England star.

The fateful day
Having moved to Latham Crescent, Dave and H would spend hours playing football in the street. Even in the early evenings when it was getting dark they would kick a ball around under the light of a lamppost. Then on that fateful day of February 6, 1958 they heard the dreadful news.

"Dad came out into the street," Dave recalls, "where we were playing, and told us that the Manchester United team had been virtually wiped out in a plane crash at Munich Airport. The news had come over on the radio. It was one of those moments you never forget, like the day President Kennedy was shot.

"I am an ardent West Bromwich Albion supporter but Manchester United held a special interest for me, and not just because of Duncan. They were *the* glamour team of the day. They were the famous Busby Babes.

"We heard that Duncan was still alive, though badly injured. Everybody was hoping he would recover. It was a terrible time, and nobody could believe it was happening.

"H and I were again playing football when our mum came to tell us Duncan had died. We couldn't believe it. After tea I went up to dad's room and he was crying his eyes out."

Thousands of people
Duncan's funeral took place in Dudley, five days after his death, and Dave's determination to attend was, initially, thwarted. His teacher Mr Whitehouse told the headmaster Mr Butler that the youngster was totally engrossed in Duncan and asked if he could have the day off school. At first the head said no because Dave was too young, but then he suggested he could go if Mr Whitehouse would drive him there in his car.

Dave takes up the story: "The streets of Dudley were lined

with thousands of people and we managed to get a spot in the High Street outside a shop called Cooks, just down from Top Church.

"There were 26 cars in the funeral cortege stretching through the town centre. There had been a service at St Francis Church and among the mourners and pallbearers were the England captain Billy Wright, international Ronnie Clayton, with several Manchester United and Albion players like Ray Barlow. Aston Villa's Irish international winger, Peter McParland, was also there."

It was there and then that Dave's fascination with Duncan – and his collection – really took off.

"When I started my first job at the Dudley Drop Forge factory, I had cuttings and pictures of Duncan plastered all over my lathe. It wasn't long before people realised how much I idolised Duncan and they would save anything to do with him and pass them on to me," says Dave. "And in recent times you wouldn't believe how much time I have spent in the archives in Dudley and

Wolverhampton, collecting material."

His search goes on to this day. Once he bid for an original photograph signed by Duncan but had to drop out when his final offer of £380 was topped.

He has received visits from Manchester United supporters, players and staff from United's academy and has taken them on tours of the landmarks associated with Duncan's life.

He has also interviewed many people who knew and even played alongside Duncan during his schooldays.

His priceless and unique collection is highlighted in this book, not just as a tribute to Duncan but as a lasting legacy to Dave Barratt's lifelong dedication to his Black Country, footballing hero.

David Harrison

Opposite page: Dave (right) with Tommy Docherty (manager of Manchester United between 1972 and 1977) celebrating the life of Duncan Edwards on the 60th anniversary of Duncan's death. Above: Dave at the Dudley Archives where he spends most of his time researching his footballing hero.

Some people have greatness thrust upon them, others are born to be great. Duncan certainly fell into the latter category. And it all began in Dudley, in Britain's industrial heartland.

THE EARLY YEARS

Opposite page: Duncan (with ball) enjoying the admiration of his school mates, March 1950. He had just been chosen, aged 13, to play for England in the schoolboys international against Northern Ireland.

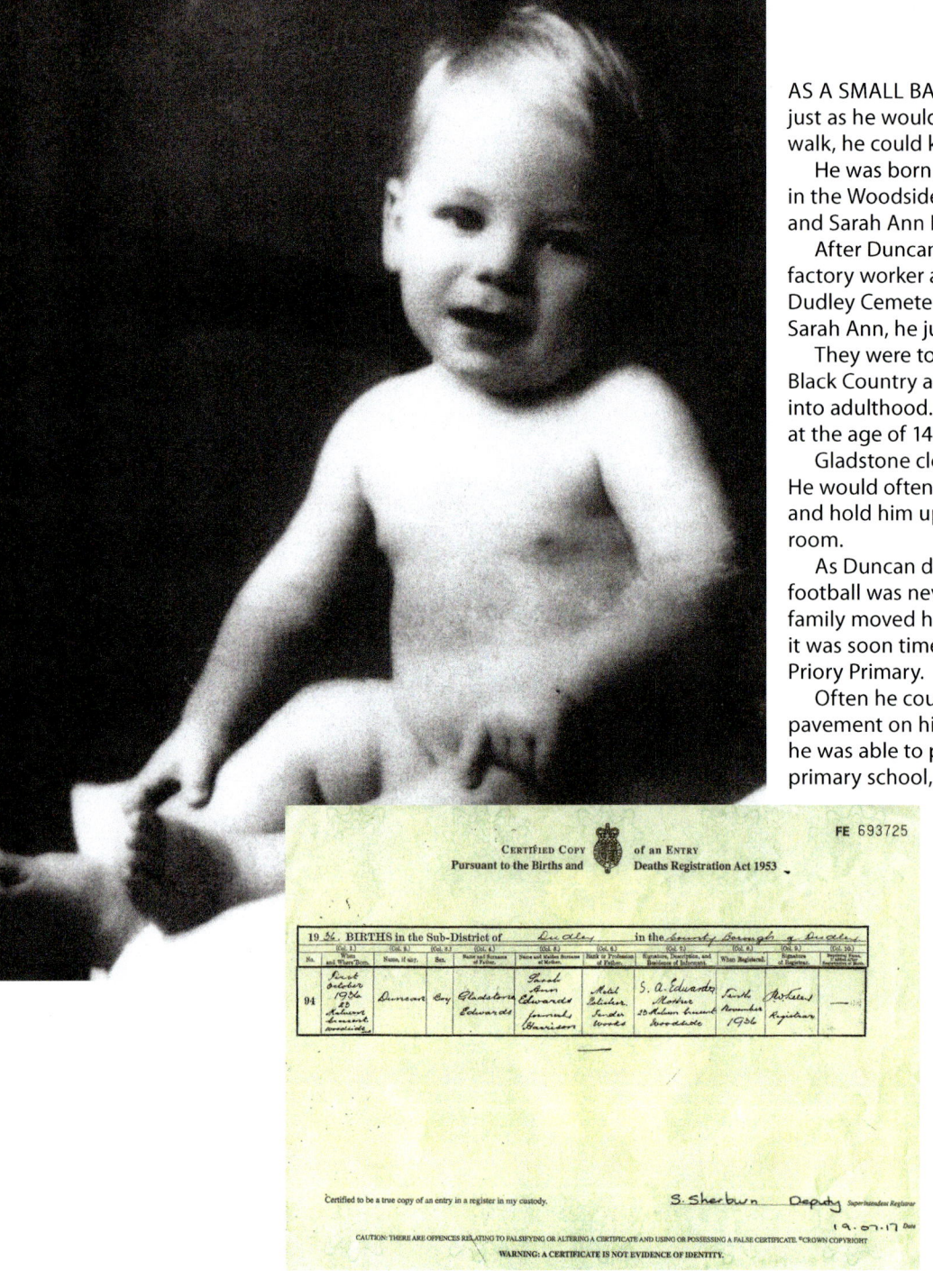

AS A SMALL BABY, Duncan Edwards stood out in a crowd, just as he would throughout his life. Even before he could walk, he could kick a football.

He was born on October 1, 1936 at 23 Malvern Crescent in the Woodside area of Dudley, the firstborn of Gladstone and Sarah Ann Edwards.

After Duncan's death Gladstone gave up his job as a factory worker and went to work sweeping up leaves at the Dudley Cemetery, where Duncan was buried. According to Sarah Ann, he just wanted to be close to Duncan.

They were tough times in this working-class area of the Black Country and Duncan was their only child to survive into adulthood. His younger sister Carol Anne died in 1947 at the age of 14 weeks.

Gladstone clearly saw some potential in baby Duncan. He would often tie some reins around the toddler's waist and hold him up as he kicked a ball up and down the living room.

As Duncan developed into a strapping youngster, a football was never too far away from his feet. After the family moved home to Elm Road on Dudley's Priory Estate, it was soon time for him to attend his first school, the Priory Primary.

Often he could be seen dribbling a ball along the pavement on his way to school and it was not long before he was able to play in more formal matches both for his primary school, from 1941 to 1948, and later for Wolverhampton Street Secondary School, from 1948 to 1952.

Duncan was on his way to becoming one of the greatest players England has ever produced.

Above left: Baby Duncan. Left: Duncan's birth certificate. Opposite page: Duncan's parents Sarah Ann and Gladstone Edwards at home at 34 Elm Road, shortly after the death of Duncan.

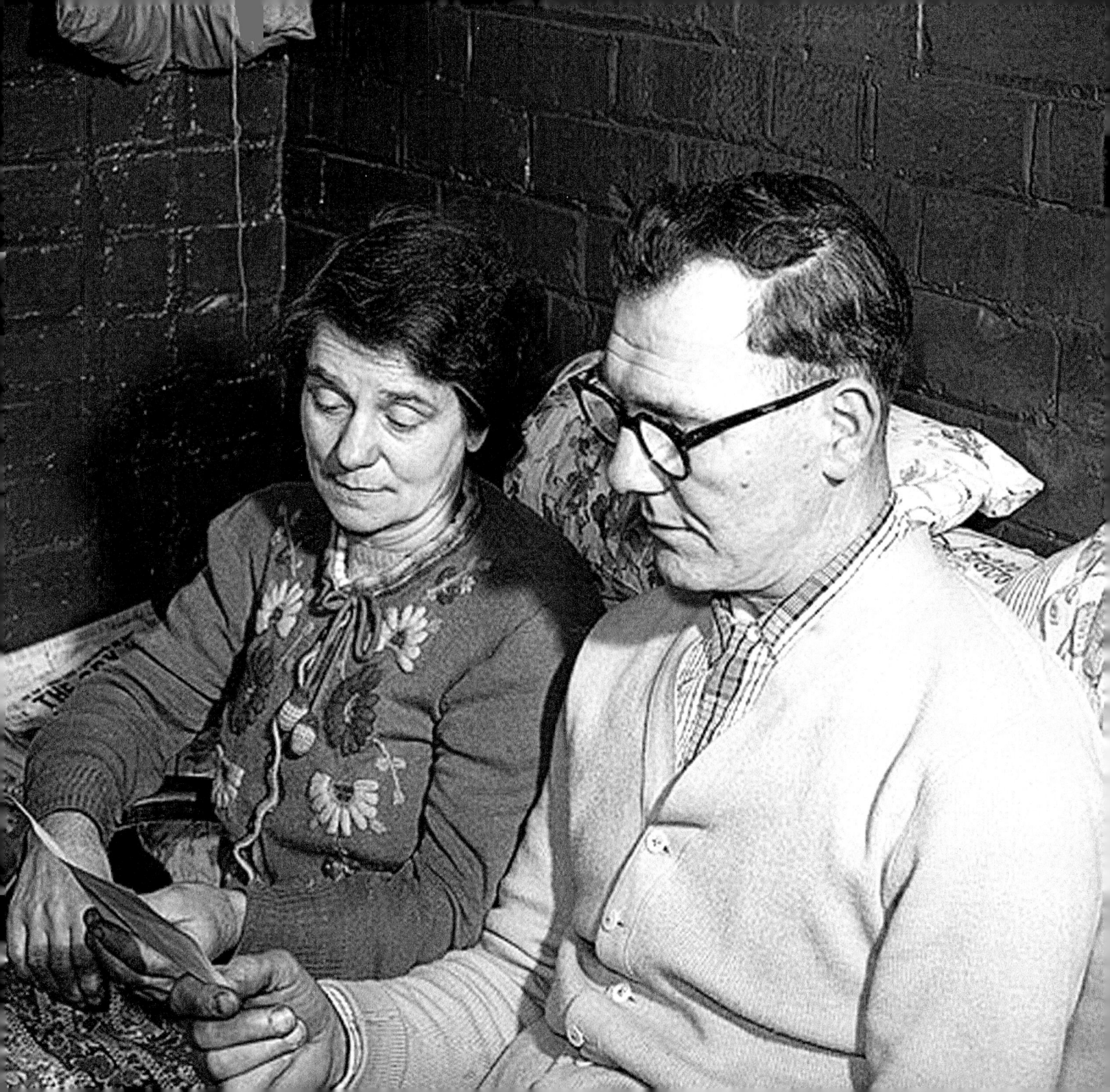

Duncan's schooldays became a vehicle for him to progress his love of football. The journey contained many achievements and led him to untold successes.

FEET FIRST AT SCHOOL

Left: Duncan's secondary school – Wolverhampton Street County Secondary Modern.

Duncan Edwards A Black Country Colossus 17

Above: Duncan's first team photo – Priory Junior School, Dudley. Duncan is third from the right on the back row.

Above: A 1949 picture of Duncan with his Wolverhampton Street School team. Duncan is front row centre with the ball.

MR GEOFF GROVES, who taught at Northfield Road Primary School, wrote of Duncan's performance after the first time he saw him play: "He played centre half amongst all these boys of 14 years of age and told them all what to do, including the referee!

"I wrote to a friend that very night and told him that I had witnessed the greatest thing ever seen in football. I added that not only would he play for the English Schools' Football Association but also he would play for the England senior side. Predictions that came true.

"There wasn't another player on the field to match him. We were all talking about him afterwards. Nobody ever really had to teach him anything about soccer.

"The game was born in him. He was a genius."

Mr Groves, who was very much involved then with the Dudley Town schoolboys' team, put Duncan in the team the following Saturday against Birmingham South.

He played for the Town side during the whole of the 1948/49 season, mostly at outside left but also at left half.

His first mention in a newspaper article was when he was 12 years and two weeks old. It was in the *Dudley Herald* and he was playing for the Dudley Boys representative team against Nuneaton Boys. Dudley won 5-2. It was played at Dudley Sports Stadium on Saturday October 16, 1948. The report describes Duncan's contribution thus:

"Edwards, the right winger, at 12 years old was the youngest player on view and was playing in only his second game as a senior.

"In the last 10 minutes Dudley monopolised the play and goals were added by Edwards, Stevens (Dennis) and Smart."

The *Herald* also featured an excellent picture of Duncan in the Dudley Schools team which lost to Kings Norton in the English Schools tournament on November 13, 1948.

Left: Duncan after his Manchester United debut against Cardiff City as a sixteen year old, on April 4, 1953.

Above: Playing in the 'Frost Trophy final' at Dudley Sports Centre, May 1949. Duncan, aged 12 years and 7 months, is second from the right, front row.

Left: Duncan made his debut for the Worcestershire Boys select team against Northamptonshire at St George's Ground, Worcester, on December 29, 1949. Duncan was 13 years and two months old. He wore the number 8 shirt and is pictured on the front row, second left. Above: A pair of leather football boots much like the boots Duncan would have worn in his youth.

Above: Duncan turned out for the England Schools team against Northern Ireland at Boundary Park, Oldham. Here he is heading the ball, second from left. Right: The match programme. Opposite page: Duncan with schoolmate Raymond Woolridge after being called up to represent England Schoolboys under-14s.

Left: The Dudley Boys team are pictured at the Sports Centre on February 17, 1951 when they beat Tamworth Boys 8-1 in a Birmingham and District Schools Shield match. Duncan is on the front row, second left. Above: Duncan scored one of the goals and here he shows his shooting power.

Duncan Edwards A Black Country Colossus

DUDLEY SCHOOLBOYS DEFEATED IN SHIELD COMPETITION

The Dudley Schools team—Back row (left to right) McConnell (St. Joseph's), O'Sullivan (St. Joseph's), Pearson (Holly Hall), Smith (Northfield Rd.), Newton (Technical College), Easthope (Halesowen Road). Front Row: Howls (Park), Smart (Park), Stevens (Rosland), Stevens (Holly Hall), captain, and Edwards (Wolverhampton Street). This same team will meet Birmingham on Saturday morning at the Sports Centre in the First Round of Birmingham and District Schools' Shield. Kick off 10.30 a.m.

Dudley made a gallant effort to earn the right to qualify for the next round of the English Schools' Shield competition when they met King's Norton in a second round re-play at the Sports Centre on Saturday, but the visitors, showing peak form, ran out winners by 3—1.

The Dudley forward line was much in the picture in the opening phase of the game and two near-scoring attempts were made by Stevens and O'Sullivan, but King's Norton gradually wrested the initiative from the home team and went ahead through Wooding. A minute before the interval Howlett, King's Norton leader, scored from a penalty awarded for hands.

Despite a promising spell of attacking by the Dudley forward line, King's Norton went further ahead soon after the interval with an unusual goal. Smith, the home goalkeeper, ran out to clear and kicked the ball against McConnell, the right-back, and it rebounded into the net.

Dudley's goal was obtained by Stevens (Rosland).

Left: The Dudley Boys team were beaten in the English Schools Shield competition 3-1 by Kings Norton in a second round replay at Dudley Sports Centre, on November 13, 1948. Duncan was 12 years old. Duncan is pictured front row far right. Above: The newspaper match report.

Opposite page: The Mayor of Dudley, Councillor George Marlow, makes a special award to Duncan on May 17, 1952 of a travelling case and accessories in recognition of the honour he brought to Dudley. Also pictured is Duncan's headmaster at Wolverhampton Street School, Mr T L Perry. Above: England Schoolboys, 1952. Duncan is fourth from the left with ball, front row. (Photo courtesy of Duncan Edwards United).

Above: Duncan (left, in football strip), aged 14 years, three months.

Left: Duncan is in the front row with ball, aged 13 years, seven months, May 16, 1950 – Wolverhampton Street School team (Collins Cup winners).

WEDNESDAY, DECEMBER 23, 2020

Football legend's Christmas t

by DAN SHAW

WHEN we printed this photograph last month, in Bugle 1474, November 25, we had no idea of how significant it was. Not until reader Dave Barratt called to tell us that he was certain Black Country football legend Duncan Edward was among the kids gathered around Santa's sleigh.

As a schoolboy, Dave was among the crowds of mourners that lined the streets of Dudley for the funeral of Duncan Edwards in 1958. Recently, Dave has devoted many hours of research at the Dudley Archives trying to find every newspaper report on the life of the tragic star, right from his early days playing school football, and trace every known photograph.

Edwards played for Dudley, Worcestershire and Birmingham schoolboys before playing for England schoolboys, Manchester United and the full national side. He died, aged 21, from the injuries he sustained in the Munich Air Disaster of 1958.

"I'm pretty certain that that is Duncan Edwards in the photograph," Dave Barratt told the Bugle. We have circled young Duncan, at the back of the crowd.

Odeon

The photograph was taken in 1950, when Duncan Edwards was 14 years old. The Odeon cinema on Castle Hill in Dudley had laid on a special treat for local children, with Santa on his sleigh.

"I'd heard that Duncan was there," said Dave, "but I didn't know there was any photograph."

The picture was passed on to the Bugle in 2001 by **Steve Edwards** of Wombourne. His mother, **Pauline Waterfield**, is in the picture – she is the tall girl in the headscarf standing beside the sleigh. Steve told us that on the day his mother, who was 13 at the time, had gone to the cinema to collect her younger brother **Bernard**, when she stumbled on Father Christmas.

Steve said: "Years after the photo was taken, my mother, who went to work as an usherette at the Odeon, was in the manager, **Mr Alexander's** office, when he kindly gave her this photograph as a gift."

70 years may have passed but Dave Barratt would

Duncan Edwards was among the children meeting Father Christmas at the Odeon Cinema, Dudley, i

Is there anyone who remembers and can confirm that Duncan Edwards was definitely in the crowd of kids at then Odeon to meet Father Christmas?
■ If you have any information please contact us at the **Black Country Bugle, Dudley Archives Centre, Tipton Road, Dudley, DY1 4SQ** or email dshaw@blackcoun

34 Duncan Edwards A Black Country Colossus

Opposite page: This photo was taken in 1950, when Duncan was 14 years old. The Odeon cinema on Castle Hill in Dudley had laid on a special treat for local children. When this photo appeared in the 'Black Country Bugle' in their November 25, 2020 edition David Barratt spotted a familiar face in the crowd. It was Duncan Edwards. David contacted the 'Bugle' and they printed this article the following week. Left: The Odeon cinema. Above: Duncan with his headmaster, Mr T L Perry.

DUNCAN'S WEMBLEY DREAM

EVEN AT A VERY young age, Duncan had his own football dreams. At the age of fifteen he wrote an essay for his teacher, Miss Stella Cook, expressing his desire to play at Wembley Stadium.

This is what he wrote: "Well it all began when I was a little boy of about seven years of age. I had heard my father takeing [sic] about a place by the name of Wembly [sic] Stadium.

"It was a wet day in April and my uncle Gorge [sic] and dad were sitting round the fire when my uncle Gorge [sic] said to my father, 'I see England are playing Scotland at Wembly [sic] next Saterday [sic].' 'Are they?' my father replied.

"I thought to myself, now's my chance to ask where this Wembly [sic] Stadium is.

"It is situated in London," my uncle said.

"I told my uncle I wish I could go there and he said I would before long. I was thirteen and still wanted to go to Wembly [sic] and on 1st of April, I was picked to play for England against Wales (at Wembly [sic] Stadium). My uncle was right when he said I would, some day, go to Wembly [sic] Stadium."

Far left: Duncan's essay describing how he dreams of playing for England at Wembley. Left: Duncan's teacher, Stella Cook. Opposite page: Duncan (second from right) realises his dream, playing at Wembley against Scotland in 1955. The Duke of Gloucester is shaking hands with goalkeeper Bert Williams. England won 7-2.

THE LAD FROM DUDLEY

Dudley is situated in the Black Country in what was (before its rapid decline in the 1980s) Britain's industrial heartland and where Duncan Edwards was born and raised. Duncan loved his home town and wherever he went he was always happy to tell people how proud he was to be a Dudley lad.

Postcards from Alan Hughes collection.

38 Duncan Edwards A Black Country Colossus

Below: Priory Park Gardens where Duncan would kick a ball around when he was a kid.

Below: Coronation Gardens – near where Duncan lived – with Dudley Castle in the distance.

Duncan's life was football, particularly at school, but there were other extracurricular activities he embarked on in his youth. Here are a few examples, including a Bible class, Morris dancing and hop picking.

THE OTHER SIDE OF DUNCAN

Left: Bert Bissell's Bible class, Vicar Street, Dudley, April 1950. Duncan is seated right, middle row. This photograph was taken six days before Duncan won his first junior England cap playing against Ireland at Boundary Park, Oldham, May 1950.

Duncan Edwards A Black Country Colossus

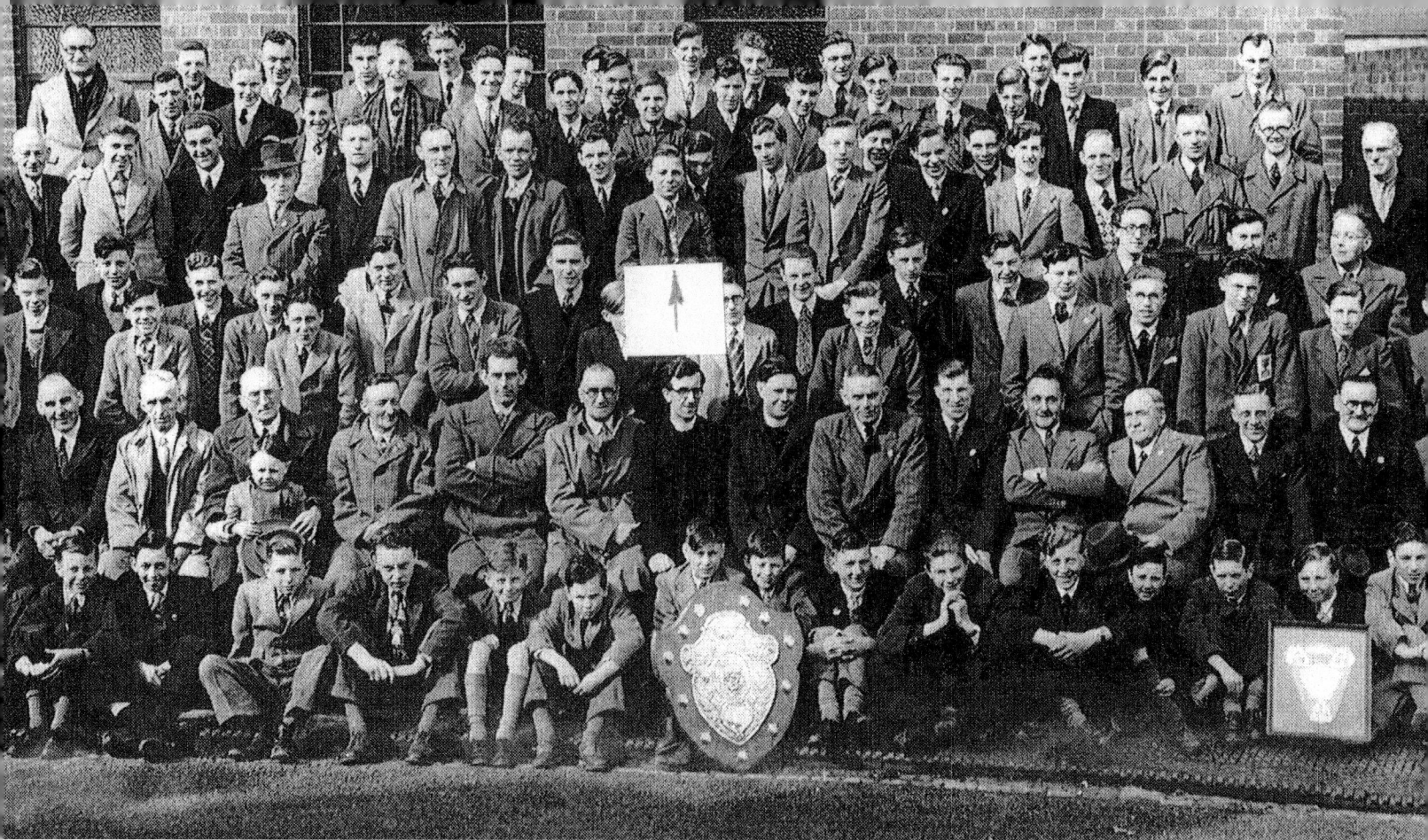

DUNCAN PLAYED FOR Wolverhampton Street School as well as for Dudley Schools, Worcestershire and Birmingham and District teams but it was not just at football that he showed exceptional skills with his feet.

He also represented his school at Morris dancing. He was selected to compete in the National Morris and Sword Dancing Festival but was also offered a trial for the English Schools Football Association's under-14 team, which fell on the same day. It is no surprise he chose the football option.

Not everyone warmed to his dancing prowess, however. Many years later, the weekly newspaper, the *Black Country Bugle*, published a letter with the title: "Duncan's dancing was not so good."

It was from reader Del Bunce, who wrote: "Regarding Duncan Edwards, his was a familiar name in our home, and we still visit his grave regularly.

"My mom was at school with Duncan and they were paired up as partners in the school Morris dancing team. The stories Mum used to tell of him being a fantastic footballer and a lovely person, but, as Mum used to recall, his skills with his stick in Morris dancing weren't quite as good as his football skills and she would go home most days with bruised and battered hands."

Duncan's life away from football also took him to a regular Bible class at Vicar Street Methodist Church under the jurisdiction of Bert Bissell, a legendary Dudley character, who dedicated his life to world peace and climbed Ben Nevis dozens of times to raise money for his charities.

DUDLEY SCHOLARS IN FOLK DANCES FROM ALL OVER THE WORLD

Above: Folk dances from around the world were included in a demonstration of country, Morris and sword dancing by pupils of Wolverhampton Street School in March 1950. In the foreground of the picture, wearing cap and gown, is 13-year-old Duncan. Opposite page: Bert Bissell's Bible class, Vicar Street, Dudley, April 1950. The arrow points to the young Duncan.

PEOPLE CAME FROM The Black Country and the Welsh Valleys to fields in Worcestershire and Herefordshire to pick hops. Women, children, and unemployed men would come to earn some money for a few weeks, as well as have an opportunity to spend time in the countryside.

These visits were very welcome for teenagers like Duncan as an escape from the smoke-filled atmosphere of the Black Country.

Hops used for the brewing of beer were in high demand back then.

Left: Hop picking near Ledbury, Herefordshire, September 1951. A tousle-haired, 14-year-old Duncan is far left, back row.

DUNCAN PLAYED IN HIS first match on Grange Park, Dudley, in September 1948. He was aged 11 years, 11 months, playing for Wolverhampton Street School against Northfield Road School. It was an outstanding performance by the young Duncan, who dominated the game against boys two years older than himself.

From 1967 to 1972 I played football for a local team called Castle Olympic. Our home ground was Grange Park.

Very little has changed since Duncan played there though the wooden hut, used as a changing room, has long gone.

The pitch was set in pleasant surroundings, but the surface was hardly the best. In winter it was often a mudbath, or frozen over, and in early summer it was baked concrete hard. Controlling the ball was a major challenge.

But I have some great personal memories of games played on the Grange, in all kinds of conditions.

One particular Saturday afternoon, on a cold winter's day, we were due to play our local rivals Dudley St James. On arrival at the ground the pitch was covered in a blanket of deep snow. The prospects of us playing didn't look good.

But everyone was keen to play and the players spent a long time trying to convince the referee it was possible. He inspected the pitch several times unable, it seemed, to make a decision.

Fortunately the ground was soft underfoot which meant it wasn't dangerous. The referee finally declared he was prepared to go ahead with the game if we were willing to sweep, and expose, the pitch markings.

So there we were, twenty-two grown men, brushing snow from a football pitch, all so we could kick a ball around for 90 minutes. And after all that effort we managed to win 1-0!

But it was such a privilege to know I had played football on the pitch that the great Duncan had played on in his youth!

David Barratt

Left: On a nostalgic visit to Grange Park. I'm standing on the football pitch – shorn of markings and goalposts, 4 May 2018. Inset: Duncan in his Manchester United days.

Duncan Edwards A Black Country Colossus 47

CHARLES BUCHAN'S FOOTBALL MONTHLY

CHARLES BUCHAN'S FOOTBALL MONTHLY began in September 1951 and changed the face of football journalism. The first words written were: 'Our objective is to provide a publication that will be worthy of our national game and the grand sportsmen who play and watch it.'

And so it proved. The first issue cost 7½p (one shilling and sixpence in old money). The magazine ran for just under 23 years, its last issue was published in June 1974.

I loved it as a kid. I couldn't wait to get the latest issue, saved for with my meagre pocket money. And at the end of each year I would buy Charles Buchan's Soccer Gift Book. Sadly, over the years, for one reason or another, they all disappeared. But in recent times I have made it my mission to collect them again. And what wonderful memories they bring back!

Alan Hughes

THE ISSUE ABOVE is dated March 1958, just three weeks after the Munich air disaster. The cover, showing Duncan, had already been printed prior to Duncan's death but after consultation and co-operation with his family it was decided that the issue should be published. Needless to say, it has become a prized collector's item.

Duncan Edwards A Black Country Colossus 49

SOCCER EXPERTS SAY—

extra energy makes the difference!

DUNCAN EDWARDS
Manchester United's great discovery and, at 18, the youngest player for fifty years to win a full cap for England, says:

"Playing in top gear until the final whistle can really take it out of you. That's why I find 'Dextrosol' Glucose Tablets so handy. They're a natural source of energy you can rely on, anytime, anywhere."

Dextrosol
gives extra energy

To produce energy, your body burns fuel. A doctor will tell you that glucose is the fuel manufactured by your body from the food you eat. 'Dextrosol' is pure glucose: the quick, *natural* source of energy. 'Dextrosol' requires no digestion but passes straight into your bloodstream, carrying energy at once to muscles, nerves and brain.

To build up energy for that extra effort, to replace energy after exertion, eat delicious 'Dextrosol' Glucose Tablets. The handy packets slip easily into your pocket. 'Dextrosol' is the natural way of renewing energy—it can do you nothing but good, and there's no limit to the amount you can eat.

For extra energy—whenever you need it!

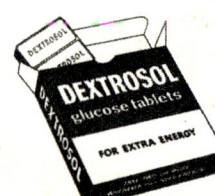

Look for the handy red and green packets, 10½d and 6d. Buy a packet today— 'Dextrosol' Glucose Tablets are now available at chemists and grocers everywhere!

DEXTROSOL BRAND glucose tablets

MADE BY THE PHARMACEUTICAL DIVISION OF BROWN & POLSON LTD.

"DEXTROSOL GIVES EXTRA ENERGY!"

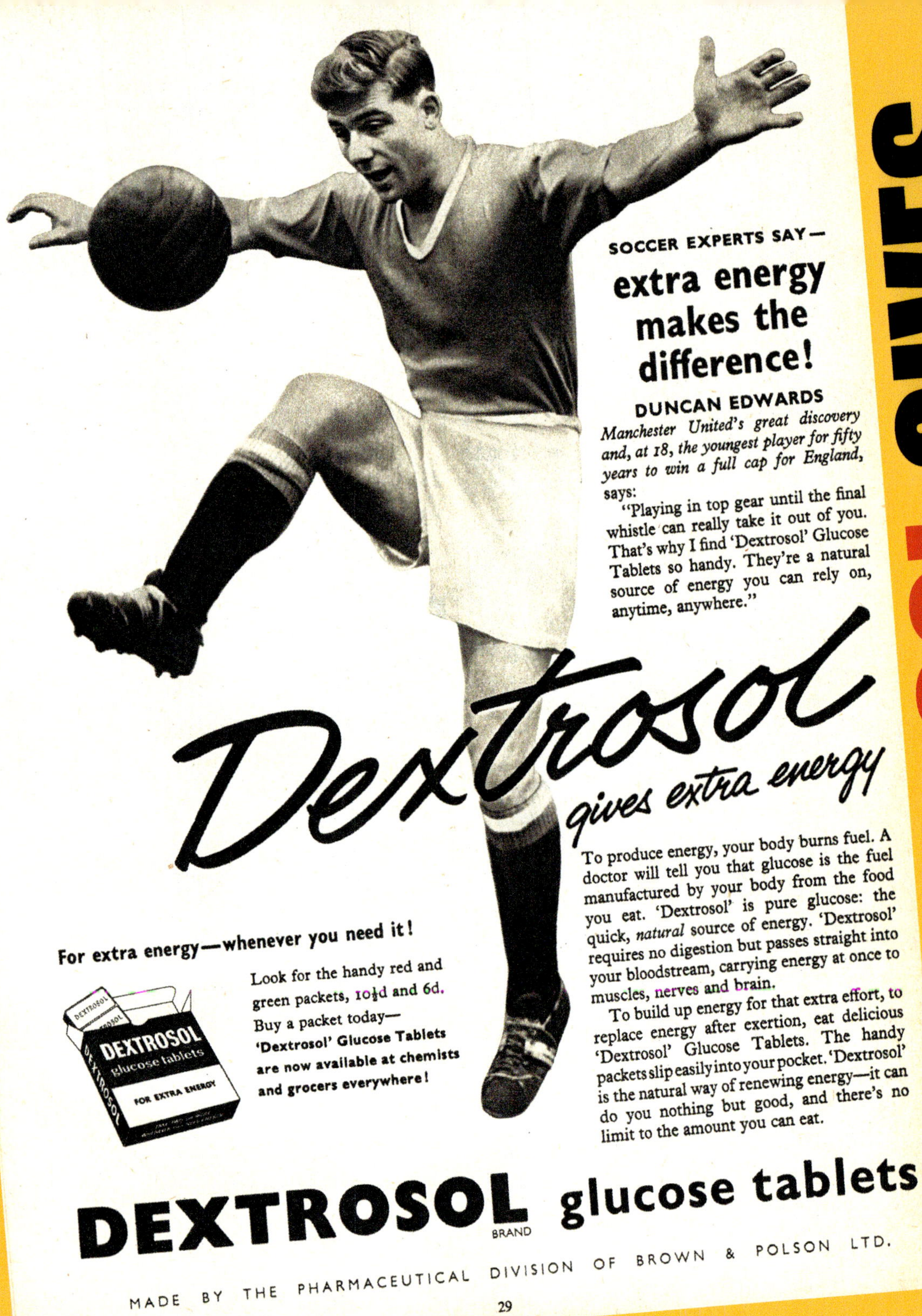

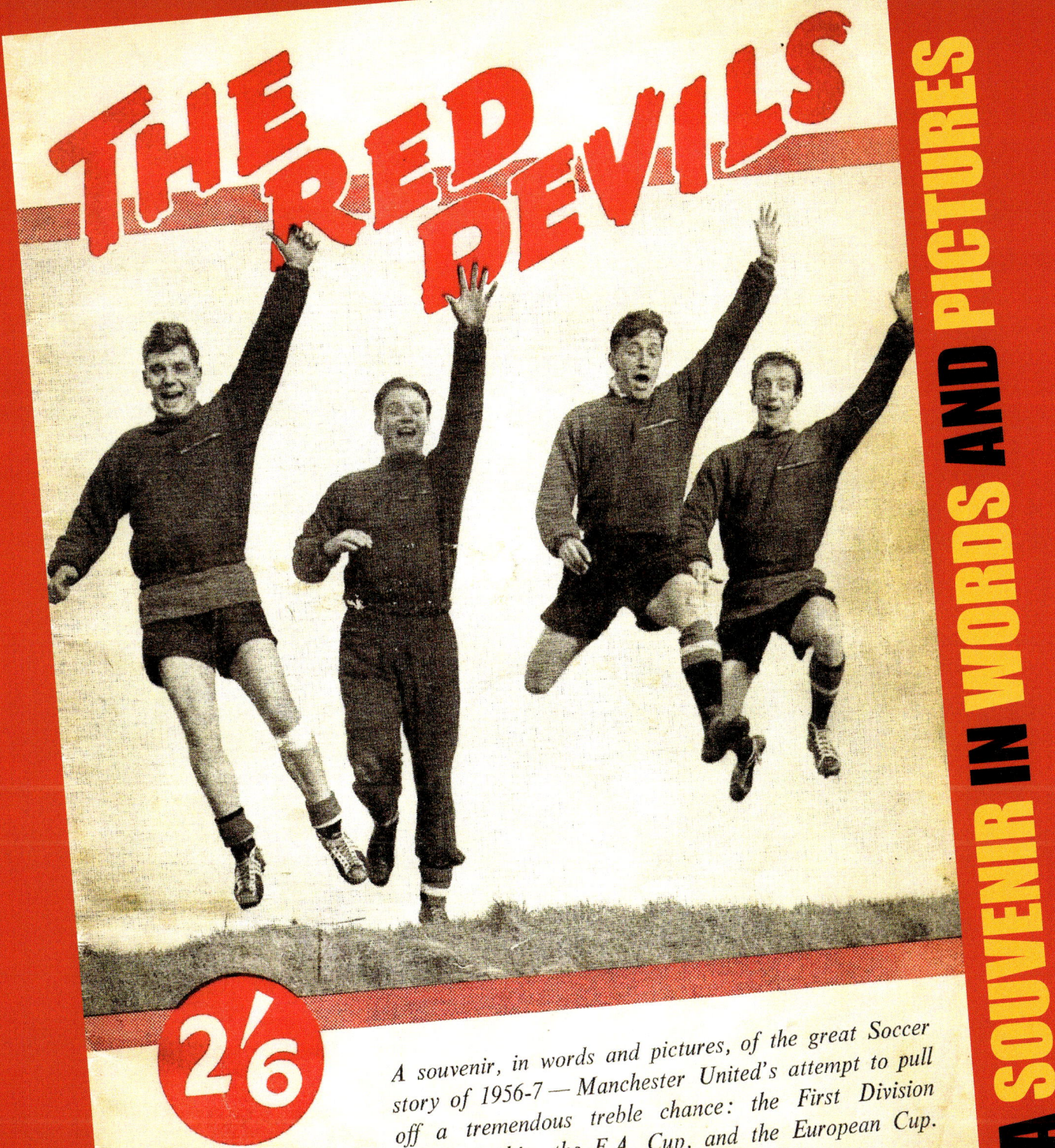

Duncan's dream came true when he became a Manchester United player. He cherished the idea of playing for the club from a very early age.

THE BUSBY BABES

Left: United won the First Division title in the 1955-56 season when most of their players were in their late teens or early twenties. They finished 11 points ahead of their nearest rivals Blackpool and Wolves. Back row (left to right), Eddie Colman, Liam Whelan, Mark Jones, Ray Wood, Ian Greaves, Duncan Edwards. Front: Johnny Berry, Roger Byrne, Dennis Viollet, Tommy Taylor, David Pegg.

Duncan Edwards A Black Country Colossus

DUNCAN PLAYED IN EVERY England schoolboy international fixture for three seasons, and was even made England captain at just fourteen years old. That record of playing for three successive seasons for England schoolboys still stands today, as does his being the youngest ever captain.

By then he was attracting a lot of attention from professional clubs. All the big Midlands clubs were prominent, Wolves, Albion, Villa, Birmingham, as well as the big London clubs, Arsenal, Tottenham Hotspur, and Chelsea.

It was the much-travelled Joe Mercer who set Duncan off down the road to Old Trafford. In 1950, Mercer, then still playing for Arsenal, was doing some coaching with the England schoolboy team. After a game between United and Arsenal, Joe happened to remark to his friend Matt Busby what a remarkable talent he had seen in the England schoolboys' team, and that in his opinion "young Edwards is going to be some player".

This alerted Busby, who sent his trusted chief scout, Joe Armstrong, down to Dudley to watch the young Edwards play. After just ten minutes, Armstrong had seen enough, and recommended that Busby should go and watch this young man himself.

The following week, both Matt and his assistant Jimmy Murphy travelled secretively to Dudley. They too, did not have to stay for too long watching Duncan play, and on the way back to Manchester Busby told Jimmy that they must not miss out on Duncan.

For two years they kept a watchful eye on the young giant. Eventually Duncan signed for Manchester United, and that was due largely to the coach, Bert Whalley. Reg Priest, the United scout in the West Midlands, had informed United that there was pressure on Duncan to sign for one of the Midland clubs or Bolton Wanderers.

Bert Whalley decided immediately to drive down to the Edwards' home in Dudley and clinch the deal for Manchester United. His journey was interrupted by his car breaking down. At 2am on the morning of June 2, 1952, a bleary-eyed Gladstone Edwards came downstairs to answer the knocking on the front door of his home.

Waiting there were Bert Whalley and Jimmy Murphy. He invited

Continued overleaf

Opposite page: Duncan, with Matt Busby, signs as a professional in 1953. Right: On 4 April 1953 Duncan played in a First Division match against Cardiff City, which United lost 4-1. He was aged just 16 years and 185 days, and became the youngest player ever to play in the top flight of English football.

both men into the living room, and called for Sarah Ann. Gladstone told both men that the decision would be left to Duncan as to which club he would like to join.

It was a foregone conclusion. Duncan arrived in the living room wearing his pyjamas, rubbing the sleep out of his eyes and immediately upon recognising the two men said:

"What's all the fuss about? I've already said there's only one club that I want to play football for, and that's Manchester United. I'd give anything to sign for them."

He had followed the exploits of the Manchester United team which had won the FA Cup in 1948, the First Division Championship in 1952, and who had also finished runners-up in the league on four other occasions. Their brand of football had captivated him. He was an undisguised United fan.

Within minutes of meeting Bert Whalley and Jimmy Murphy, Duncan signed the forms to become a Manchester United player. A few days later he moved into digs in Stretford and began his career in professional football.

When he arrived at Manchester's London Road Station, Duncan was met by Bert Whalley, who took him past Old Trafford and down Warwick Road to the home of Mrs. Watson at 5 Birch Avenue. She would become his landlady and second mother during his time at Old Trafford.

A multitude of games

The start of his career as a United player was nothing short of sensational. In the second round of the Youth Cup in 1952 he broke his duck against an unfortunate Nantwich, hitting five goals in United's overwhelming 23-0 victory.

His performance shocked even the most experienced journalists. One newspaper reporter, Edgar Turner, wrote: "He is big and almost as strong as a man and I cannot recall one pass, long or short, by Edwards that could not be described to conjure up a phrase from the past such as a daisy cutter.

"His delivery of the ball to his forwards, even from well back, was equal to the best I have seen anywhere, league games and internationals included, for a very long time.

"When I say his tackling was strong and his covering excellent it is still not the end of the story. He also scored five goals!"

Duncan played a multitude of games during his first season – turning out for the colts, the A team, the youth team and the reserves.

In April 1953, he was called into the office of Matt Busby and told, "Go and get your football boots, son, you're playing for the first team tomorrow." He was only 16 years old and still an amateur.

Something special

He was to make his first team debut in the number six shirt against Cardiff City. Duncan was later to comment: "Making my Football League debut was not terrifying for me as many people thought, after having played at Wembley three times before I was fifteen".

The following season, 1953-54, began in something of a disappointing fashion for Manchester United – they won only four of their opening fifteen games. Matt Busby decided to make changes to his somewhat ageing side.

For the away trip to Huddersfield Town, he decided to keep Jackie Blanchflower and Dennis Viollet in the side following their promising displays against Kilmarnock, with Duncan, who had recently signed professional forms, retaining the number six jersey, giving the side a rather youthful look.

The trio of youngsters Viollet, Blanchflower and Edwards slotted well into the team and adapted comfortably to the pace of First Division football. The game ended in a 0-0 draw but it heralded the start of something special.

This was the headline in the *Manchester Evening News* that night: "Busby's Bouncing Babes Keep All Town Awake." And so the Busby Babes were born and christened.

By the time he died at Munich Duncan had featured in the United first team for six seasons, amassed 177 senior appearances, won two league titles, two Charity Shields, played in an FA Cup final, picked up eighteen England caps (as the youngest to play for England in the 20th century) and was voted third in the 1957 European Player of the Year award behind Alfredo Di Stefano.

Opposite page: Duncan, relaxed and smiling for the camera.
Right: Duncan, right, playing in the 1957 FA Cup final against Aston Villa, as emergency keeper Jackie Blanchflower (Ray Wood was injured) catches a high ball.

Above: The United youth team played in a tournament in Bangor, Northern Ireland, in the 1953-54 season and stayed at the Hotel Pickie. Back row (left to right) Ian Greaves, Walter Whitehurst, Tommy Barratt, Gordon Clayton, Alan Rhodes, Paddy Kennedy, Brace Fulton, hotel manager (name unknown), Middle row, left to right, Eddie Lewis, Bill Inglis (trainer), Jimmy Murphy, Bert Whalley, Noel McFarlane. Front row, (left to right) Sammy Chapman, Eddie Colman, Duncan Edwards, Billy Whelan, Albert Scanlon.

Above: Duncan (front right) sits down for a meal in his digs. For his entire career at Manchester United he lived in similar accommodation, sharing a room and the dining table with his team-mates.

Left: Duncan was full of admiration for Matt Busby, the man who fulfilled his United dreams. Here the United manager gathers the players for an informal team talk. Duncan is fourth from the right. Above: Skill and power in those formidable thighs.

Manchester United's youth team, August 1952, with Duncan second from the right on the back row.

Above: A rare fully-signed photo of the United team with Duncan second from the left in between goalkeeper Ray Wood and centre forward Tommy Taylor.

Left: Duncan and Roger Byrne with the assuring presence of Matt Busby. Below: Duncan with a 21st birthday card. Opposite page: Duncan (far right) out for a pre-training session stroll with teammates (from left to right) Mark Jones (half-hidden), Dennis Viollet, Jackie Blanchflower and Bill Foulkes.

Left: Duncan never lost sight of where he was from and was always willing to accommodate the fans. Here he is signing an autograph at his last league game before the Munich disaster – against Arsenal at Highbury on February 1, 1958.

Right: It's a muddy old game. Duncan ready for an after-match bath with Dennis Viollet, Roger Byrne and Eddie Colman. Opposite page: Power and balance. Duncan was just as comfortable with both feet and here he shows his left-foot skills.

Duncan Edwards A Black Country Colossus 67

Opposite page: The Busby Babes, Division One Champions 1957, displaying the trophy. Duncan is in front, bottom left. Above: Team photo of the champions, Duncan is the player far right, middle row.

BOBBY AND DUNCAN

Charles Buchan's FOOTBALL MONTHLY

JUNE 1962

1/6
Overseas price 2/-
Forces overseas 1/6

BOBBY CHARLTON
Manchester United and England

INSIDE: ENGLAND'S WORLD CUP HOPES

BOBBY CHARLTON completed his National Service alongside Duncan and they played together for Manchester United. Bobby said: "Duncan was my best friend, my team mate and the greatest footballer I ever saw."

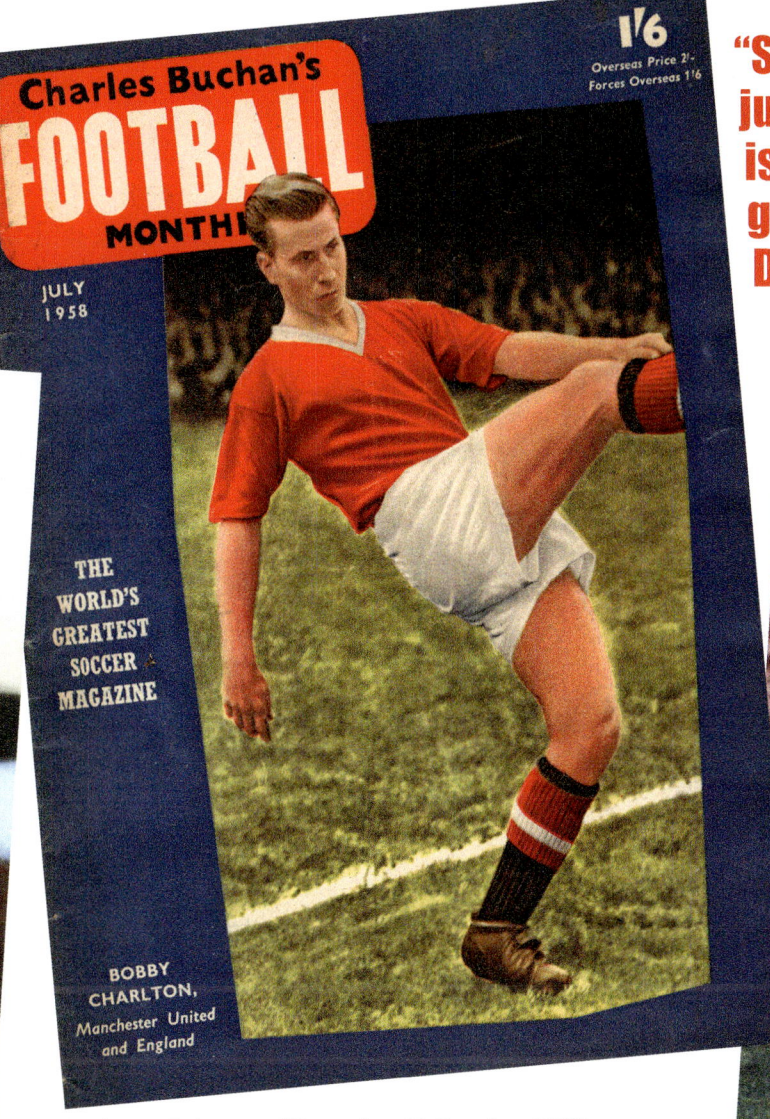

"Sentiment can throw a man's judgement out of perspective. Yet it is not the case with him. A few are great and they deserve respect. But Duncan Edwards was the greatest."

Bobby Charlton

In the early hours of Saturday, 21 October, 2023 **BOBBY CHARLTON** died. He was 86 years old and had been suffering with dementia. Manchester United said Bobby ranked as "one of the greatest and most beloved players in the history of our club. He was admired as much for his sportsmanship and integrity as he was for his outstanding qualities as a footballer. His fellow 1966 World Cup winning teammate Geoff Hurst said, "We will never forget him and nor will all of football."

Duncan Edwards A Black Country Colossus

DUNCAN IN GREAT COMPANY

Duncan, only 21 years old when he died, was already regarded as a great footballer. When you consider the sort of quality players who were around at the time it beggars belief as to how good Duncan was. Here are just some of his esteemed contemporaries.

Left: **DANNY BLANCHFLOWER** played for Northern Ireland and captained Tottenham Hotspur, including during their double-winning season of 1960-61. Blanchflower said of football: "The great fallacy is that the game is first and last about winning. It is nothing of the kind. The game is about glory, it is about doing things in style and with a flourish, about going out and beating the lot, not waiting for them to die of boredom."

Above: **BILLY WRIGHT** spent his entire club career at Wolverhampton Wanderers and was the first footballer in the world to earn 100 international (England) caps.

Left: **JOHNNY HAYNES** played most of his career at Fulham and made 56 appearances for his country. Nicknamed 'The Maestro', his attacking play was noted for two-footed passing ability, vision and deftness of touch.

Above: **TOM FINNEY** was a winger or centre forward for Preston North End and England. He is widely acknowledged to have been one of England's greatest-ever players. He was noted for his loyalty to Preston, for whom he made 433 Football League and 39 FA Cup appearances, scoring a total of 210 goals. He played for England 76 times, scoring 30 goals.

STANLEY MATTHEWS (Blackpool), the wizard of dribble, has the ball under complete control during this run in from the touch line.

Above: Known as 'The Wizard of Dribble', **STANLEY MATTHEWS** retired in 1965, aged 50. He had made nearly 700 League appearances for Blackpool and Stoke City. He was also capped 84 times for England, including wartime internationals. He was the first winner of both the European Footballer of the Year and the Football Writers' Association Footballer of the Year awards.

"Every football manager goes through his life looking for one great player and praying he'll find one. Just one. I was luckier than most, I found two – Duncan Edwards and George Best."

Matt Busby

There was never any doubt that Duncan would play for the full England side and indeed he was fully expected to captain his country at some stage.

THE CAP FITS
PLAYING FOR ENGLAND

Opposite page: England line-up, back row (left to right), Ronnie Clayton, Don Howe, Eddie Hopkinson, Derek Kevan, Duncan Edwards, Roger Byrne. Front row, Bryan Douglas, Tommy Taylor, Billy Wright, Johnny Haynes, Tom Finney.

TWO YEARS AFTER becoming the youngest player to appear in a first team game, Duncan became the youngest England debutant at 18 years and 183 days old, a record eventually beaten by Michael Owen.

He played at left half, in a 7-2 victory in a Home Championship game against Scotland in April 1955. One Press report proclaimed: "Powerfully built, he showed strength and determination in defence and the ability to open up the game with long, accurate passes."

He went on to play in four matches of the successful 1958 World Cup qualifying campaign, although Munich denied him the opportunity to play in the tournament finals in Sweden.

Many observers felt that had Duncan survived the Munich crash, he would have been in his prime, at 29, during the 1966 World Cup, when England beat Germany 4-2, and he would have been lifting the cup rather than West Ham's Bobby Moore.

Above: Duncan playing for England against Scotland. Opposite page: Duncan training at Highbury with legends Stanley Matthews (left) and Billy Wright ahead of England's game against Scotland in April 1957.

Opposite page: England Under-23s ready to board their flight to Bucharest in 1957. Back (left to right): Duncan Edwards, David Pegg. Middle: Ronnie Clayton, Alan Hodgkinson. Front: Johnny Haynes and manager Walter Winterbottom. The game saw England win 1-0 with Haynes scoring the winner. This page, main photo: Duncan's first England cap. Left: Duncan wearing an England Scoolboys cap. He made his debut for them on May 6, 1950, aged 13. Above right: Duncan getting ready to play for England at Wembley with Tom Finney next to him.

FALLING IN LOVE

DUNCAN WAS ENGAGED to be married to Molly Leech, who was 22 years old and worked in the offices of a textile machine manufacturer in Altrincham.

The couple met at a function in a hotel at Manchester Airport after being introduced by a mutual friend. They dated for a year before becoming engaged, sadly just days before the Munich disaster.

They would have most likely wed at the end of the following football season. They were godparents to the daughter of Molly's friend Josephine Stott.

After Duncan's death, Molly moved to Weston-Super-Mare to live with her brother. Eventually she married a semi-professional footballer and gave birth to two daughters. She returned to Manchester twice a year to visit friends but she would never discuss Duncan or Munich. Molly eventually emigrated to America and died in September 2004.

Far left: Duncan with Molly, the love of his life. Left: This photo of Duncan was found in Molly's purse.

Duncan Edwards A Black Country Colossus

Duncan Edwards tackled any challenge head-on and it was no different when his Manchester United career was interrupted by a spell of National Service.

YOU'RE IN THE ARMY NOW

Left: Duncan in his Royal Army Ordnance Corps uniform sitting next to his collection of England caps.

THE 1954-55 ENGLISH FOOTBALL season had only just been consigned to the record books when Duncan Edwards received his call-up papers to join the Royal Army Ordnance Corps.

So off he went to Nesscliffe Central Ammunition Depot, near Shrewsbury, to tackle the drills and Army disciplines, with the same energy and enthusiasm he used when dealing with his many football challenges.

Another player who was to find himself alongside Duncan during those Army days was the familiar figure of Bobby Charlton, who related the story of how he was met by his United team mate upon arrival at the camp.

"Duncan was a year older than I was and he took charge of me the moment I arrived at the army camp. He had my billet arranged and everything. When he showed me to the billet, he noticed there was a spring sticking out of the bed, and said to me 'we can't have that.'"

"It was a great big iron bed, but he hoisted it over his shoulder, mattress, frame and all and went off in search of a better one for me."

The routine for Duncan and Bobby was usually playing for the Army team on a Wednesday and Manchester United on a Saturday. On returning to their Shropshire base by train they often missed their stop at Shrewsbury and would end up at Ludlow Station because they were so worn out. As 1955 moved into its final months, Duncan was well integrated into army life and had become a regular member of the army football team as well as fulfilling his obligations to United.

It was not uncommon for Duncan to be playing two, sometimes three games per week. Since his debut in the Army national team he had featured regularly and his performances at this level were as special to him as those in the Football League while wearing the red of United.

The Army often laid first claim to his services and on one occasion he was refused leave to play for United unless he helped his camp team progress in what was seen as a prestige cup-tie by the powers that be. On 6 June 1957 Duncan finally walked away from Nesscliffe Central Ammunition Depot after two years service.

He had played in almost 100 games of football for the Army, numerous International games and made 80 first-team appearances for Manchester United as he helped them to win consecutive First Division Championships in 1955-56 and 1956-57.

Left: The Nesscliffe Army Royal Army Ordnance Corps football team, 1957. Duncan (back row far right) is pictured with his army teammates, including his Manchester United colleague and great friend Bobby Charlton (back row third right).

Duncan Edwards A Black Country Colossus 87

Opposite page: Duncan adjusting his tie ready for parade. Above: Outside the barracks. Right: Happy to be on leave. Below: A Nissan hut at Nesscliffe Central Ammunition Depot, near Shrewsbury.

The football world still mourns the dreadful events of February 6, 1958 when the Busby Babes were cut down in their prime at Munich.

DEATH AND DISASTER AT MUNICH

Left: Manchester United players line up before their European Cup tie against Red Star in Belgrade; this was the last group photo taken of them. The next day their aeroplane crashed on take-off after refuelling at Munich airport.

Left: Manchester United line up before their European Cup tie against Red Star in Belgrade. This was the last group photo taken of them. The next day their aeroplane crashed on take-off after refuelling at Munich airport; Above: United captain Roger Byrne exchanges pennants with his opposite number, Rajko Mitić, before the game. It ended in a 3-3 draw, thus securing United's passage into the semi-final.

Left and above: The wreckage of the British European Airways plane after it crashed on the third attempt at take-off. An investigation by West German airport authorities originally blamed the pilot of the plane, Captain James Thain (inset) for the disaster, saying he did not de-ice the aircraft's wings, despite eyewitness statements indicating that de-icing was unnecessary. It was later established that the crash was caused by slush on the runway which had made it impossible for the plane to gain flying speed. Thain was cleared in 1969. He died after suffering a heart attack on August 6, 1975, at the age of 54, in Berkshire.

Above: Bodies strewn across the snow-covered runway. Opposite page: United players view the devastating scene, including Harry Gregg (left) who was considered the hero of the tragedy. Gregg risked his life to go back on board after hearing a baby crying. The child's name was Vesna Lukic, just 22 months old at the time, and Gregg carried her to safety. She was travelling with her mother, Vera, the wife of a Yugoslavian diplomat. With flames licking the side of the plane, the United keeper returned to save Vera, as well as teammates Bobby Charlton and Dennis Viollet. Gregg died in 2020, aged 87, leaving Charlton as the only remaining Munich survivor.

Manchester Even[ing]

27,654 — TV & RADIO—PAGE 2 — THURSDAY, FEBRUARY 6,

UNITED C[RASH]
CRASH: "28

Plunged into houses at M[unich]
SURVIVORS SAVED in BLAZING WRECKAGE

ONE of the greatest disasters to befall British football struck Manchester United this afternoon when the plane carrying the £350,000 wonder team crashed [at] Munich. At least 28 of the 40 aboard were killed; some reports said higher casualties were feared.

The plane, a B.E.A. Elizabethan, had just taken

United players and other [members of the party board...]

News

LATE FINAL

PRICE 3d.

P XI

DIE"

ch, exploded

We will remember them...

BENT COLMAN

JONES WHELAN

TAYLOR PEGG

ROGER BYRNE

DUNCAN EDWARDS

DESPITE the many thousands of words that have been written about the terrible air disaster on February 6 that cut down so many Manchester United players and officials, I find it difficult to realise they will no longer delight us with their skill and courage.

United had become world-famous, even to a greater extent than Arsenal in their palmy years. They owed a great deal to the sportsmanship, the ability and the team spirit of great men like Roger Byrne, Geoffrey Bent, Eddie Colman, Mark Jones, Bill Whelan, Tommy Taylor, David Pegg, and Duncan Edwards.

To the relatives of these lovable young men who lost their lives I extend, on behalf of many "Football Monthly" readers who have asked me to do so, and my staff, our deepest sympathy. May time heal the deep wounds inflicted.

And to those United members severely injured, like Matt Busby and Johnny Berry, I sincerely hope they will soon be restored to complete health; and that before long they will be able to take up life's threads where they were broken.

To me personally, it has been a great shock. I had seen them, at Highbury the previous Saturday, give a wonderful exhibition of Soccer, one of the best for many years. I thought then, United, blossoming further with more experience, would become the finest Soccer machine of the century.

Adding to the shock was the loss of so many journalistic friends with whom I had travelled to many corners of the earth and spent so many happy hours.

They were able men who wrote about the game and players without fear or favour.

Since the war, Manchester United have been without rival in League, F.A. Cup and European Cup.

It was a team of experts playing for the good of the side as a whole. And now some of those experts have passed away, their parts in the victory plan will not be overlooked or forgotten.

England, too, will sorely miss the artistry and wholehearted work of Byrne, Edwards and Taylor.

I have been in the company of these outstanding players many times. Their modest, unassuming behaviour was a credit to their club and to their country.

Every day that passes, I receive messages of sympathy from all over the world. I pass them on to United officials with a sad heart. With the memorial words of former heroes: *"At the going down of the sun and in the morning, we will remember them."*

CHARLES BUCHAN.

Left: The 'Manchester Evening News' front-page report of the disaster.
Above: 'We will remember them' – a tribute to the Busby Babes who died in the crash, Charles Buchan's Football Monthly, March 1958.

• Manchester United were due to play Wolves immediately after the crash on February 8. The fixture was postponed. The match-day programme had already been printed with the names of the dead players printed in the team line-ups. Most of the programmes were pulped but some slipped through the net and have been sold at auction for up to £10,000.

100 Duncan Edwards A Black Country Colossus

THE LEGEND OF THE BUSBY BABES WILL NEVER DIE

There were 44 people on board British European Airways Flight 609 when it crashed taking off in heavy snow, 20 of whom died at the scene. The injured, some unconscious, were taken to Munich's Rechts der Isar Hospital, where three more died. Below is a list of those who died and those who survived.

FATALITIES

CREW MEMBERS
Captain Kenneth Rayment. Co-pilot on the flight. He survived but suffered multiple injuries and died in hospital five weeks later as a result of brain damage.

PASSENGERS
MANCHESTER UNITED PLAYERS
Geoff Bent, Roger Byrne, Eddie Colman, Duncan Edwards (survived the crash, but died in hospital 15 days later), Mark Jones, David Pegg, Tommy Taylor, Billy Whelan

MANCHESTER UNITED STAFF
Walter Crickmer, club secretary
Tom Curry, trainer
Bert Whalley, chief coach

JOURNALISTS
Frank Swift, *News of the World* (also a former England and Manchester City goalkeeper). Donny Davies, retired footballer, who went on to write for the *Manchester Guardian*. Former *Express & Star* reporter George Follows (*Daily Herald*). Archie Ledbrooke (*Daily Mirror*). Alf Clarke (*Manchester Evening Chronicle*). Tom Jackson (*Manchester Evening News*). Eric Thompson (*Daily Mail*). Henry Rose (*Daily Express*)

SURVIVORS

CREW
Captain James Thain, pilot (died 1975)

PASSENGERS
MANCHESTER UNITED PLAYERS
Johnny Berry (never played again, died 1994)
Jackie Blanchflower (never played again, died 1998)
Bobby Charlton (died 2023)
Bill Foulkes (died 2013)
Harry Gregg (died 2020)
Kenny Morgans (died 2012)
Albert Scanlon (died 2009)
Dennis Viollet (died 1999)
Ray Wood (died 2002)

MANCHESTER UNITED STAFF
Matt Busby, manager (died 1994)

JOURNALIST
Frank Taylor, *News Chronicle* reporter (died 2002)

Opposite page: The Busby Babes left to right back row: Whitefoot, Colman, Foulkes, Wood, Byrne (captain), Blanchflower, Edwards. Front row: Berry, Whelan, Taylor, Viollett, Pegg.

More than 5,000 people lined the streets of Dudley along the route to the cemetery on the day of Duncan's funeral on February 26, 1958.

REST IN PEACE DUNCAN

Left: The hearse carrying Duncan's coffin drives past thousands of mourners in Dudley High Street. Overleaf: Duncan's coffin being carried into church. The coffin bearers included footballers Billy Wright, Ray Barlow, Don Howe, Ronnie Clayton, Peter McParland and Pat Saward.

Duncan was buried at Dudley Cemetery alongside his sister Carol Anne. His tombstone reads: "A Day of Memory, Sad to recall, Without Farewell, He left us all." The grave is permanently festooned with flowers and scarves in Manchester United colours and is visited frequently by United fans from all over the world.

IN LOVING MEMORY OF DUNCAN

Opposite page: Duncan's grave, adorned with Manchester United red, white and black. Duncan is buried with his sister, Carol Anne, who died in 1947, aged just 14 weeks. His mother Sarah Ann, who died in April 2003, is buried with her husband Gladstone in a grave that is only yards away from Duncan.

Opposite page: Matt Busby at the unveiling of the stained-glass window dedicated to Duncan in St. Francis Church, Priory Estate, Dudley, August 1961.

Left: The magnificent Duncan statue which stands proudly in Dudley High Street. Above: A Dudley street which carries Duncan's name.

Left: The Duncan Edwards pub, formerly the Wrens Nest on the Priory estate, Dudley, underwent an arson attack (May 1, 2006) and sadly the building was totally gutted. Above: Duncan's mum, Sarah Ann, sitting in the pub and enjoying a drink, underneath a framed portrait of Duncan.

Duncan Edwards A Black Country Colossus

Helping to keep Duncan's memory alive – the Duncan Edwards Leisure Centre is a new £18.2 million facility in Dudley. It was officially opened by former Manchester United player Denis Irwin on March 9, 2022. Comprising two swimming pools, sauna, sports hall, state-of-the-art gym, immersive spin studio, fitness studios, soft play, wellness suite, café and more. Facilities also cater for disabled access.

Above: Bobby Charlton at the unveiling of a blue plaque dedicated to Duncan, Priory Park, Dudley, October 1, 2016 (Photo courtesy of the 'Express & Star'). Right: Gladstone's grave. He shares his resting place with his wife, Sara Ann, just yards away from his son's grave in the graveyard on Dudley's Stourbridge Road. Opposite page: Sarah Ann with a framed photo of her beloved son.

God is with us for our Captain.

WRENS NEST BOWLING CLUB

Thanking God for the Life of Duncan Edwards, died at Munich, February 1958.

"Duncan Edwards... like a rock in a raging sea."

Stanley Matthews

Left: These stained-glass windows in St Francis Parish Church, Dudley, are a tribute to Duncan, and show him memorialised in Manchester United and England kit.

ALTHOUGH MANCHESTER UNITED supporters have been meeting at Old Trafford on 6th February each year to honour those who died in the Munich crash, it is only in recent times that singing **'THE FLOWERS OF MANCHESTER'** has become a regular occurrence.

THE FLOWERS OF MANCHESTER

THE FLOWERS OF MANCHESTER

One cold and bitter Thursday in Munich, Germany
Eight great football stalwarts conceded victory
Eight men will never play again who met destruction there
The flowers of English football,
THE FLOWERS OF MANCHESTER
Matt Busby's boys were flying, returning from Belgrade
This great United family, all masters of their trade
The pilot of the aircraft, the skipper Captain Thain
Three times they tried to take off and twice turned back again
The third time down the runway disaster followed close
There was slush upon that runway and the aircraft never rose
It ploughed into the marshy ground, it broke, it overturned
And eight of the team were killed as the blazing wreckage burned
Roger Byrne and Tommy Taylor who were capped for England's side
And Ireland's Billy Whelan and England's Geoff Bent died
Mark Jones and Eddie Colman, and David Pegg also
They all lost their lives as it ploughed on through the snow
Big Duncan he went too, with an injury to his frame
Johnny Berry and Jack Blanchflower will never play again
The great Matt Busby lay there, the father of his team
Three long months passed by before he saw his team again
The trainer, coach and secretary, and a member of the crew
Also eight sporting journalists who with United flew
And one of them Big Swifty, who we will ne'er forget
The finest English 'keeper that ever graced the net
Oh, England's finest football team its record truly great
Its proud successes mocked by a cruel turn of fate
Eight men will never play again, who met destruction there
The flowers of English football,
THE FLOWERS OF MANCHESTER

"Come on Mum, get me home. I can't miss the Wolves game on Saturday."

Duncan Edwards' mum recalls his dying words after the Munich air disaster.